POP PEOPLE™

Aaron Carter

by Michael-Anne Johns

Y0-BBD-478

SCHOLASTIC INC.

New York   Toronto   London   Auckland   Sydney   Mexico City   New Delhi   Hong Kong

*A special thank-you to my Scholastic editors Randi Reisfeld
and Michèle Rosenthal — for their help, encouragement,
and most of all . . . patience.*

Photo Credits:
Cover: Joseph Galea; Insert Page 1: Joseph Galea; Insert Page 2:
Joseph Galea; Insert Page 3: Ron Wolfson/London Features Inter-
national; Insert Page 4: Joseph Galea; Insert Page 5: Sylvain
Gaboury/DMI: Insert Page 6: Jen Lowery/London Features Interna-
tional; Insert Page 7: Ron Wolfson/London Features International;
Insert Page 8: Ron Wolfson/London Features International.

This unofficial biography is not authorized by or affiliated with
Aaron Carter.

ISBN 0-439-25417-5

12 11 10 9 8 7 6 5 4 3 2 1   0 1 2 3 4/0

Printed in the U.S.A.
First Scholastic printing, November 2000

CONTENTS

iNTRODUCTiON

All About the AMAZiNG Aaron Carter!

Fact: Aaron Carter turns thirteen years old on December 7, 2000.

Fact: Aaron Carter is a professional artist, an accomplished singer, dancer, and all-around entertainer, who is totally at home on the concert stage.

Fact: Because he started out — at the age of nine! — in Europe, he's already amassed tons of fans.

Fact: In the summer of 2000, Aaron's first single, "Aaron's Party (Come Get It)" from his first full-length American CD was released. The song hit the charts running, and the album of the same name was set for release in September.

Fact: Some people are already calling him, "the Little Prince of Pop."

Amazing? Well, yes.

And no.

Yes, because, hello — he's thirteen! And most kids his age are dealing with school, sports, relationships, parents, self-esteem, curfews . . . the usual stuff. Most kids his age aren't home-schooled, don't spend hours in recording studios, rehearsals, in front of the video cameras, answering questions for magazine writers, getting their pictures taken a zillion times.

But then there's the "no." In many ways, it's not all that amazing that this thirteen-year-old is a certified pop star. There's the whole family thing going on. As any pop-savvy fan knows, Aaron is the younger brother of the Backstreet Boys' Nick Carter. Because BSB is hyper-famous, Aaron did have an easy way to get in the showbiz door. Once there, of course, he had to "walk the walk" — that is, he had to have the musical talent, the stamina, and the ambition to be a pop star. Both, as you'll see, come very naturally to the boy.

There's another reason for the "No, it's not all that amazing." And it's actually a sort of "history of pop" reason. You might not realize it, but there are at least a few musical superstars who really did start out at Aaron's age. Donny Osmond was one, Ricky Martin is another, and Michael Jackson was, very famously, yet another. By thirteen, all three had hit songs, and were teenage idols. Decades later, all three are still making music and showbiz news.

No one without a crystal ball knows how it'll all shake out for Aaron, but how it all began, what he's doing now, and who he really is, you're about to find out.

CHAPTER 1

Aaron Carter

Aaron Charles Carter is barely into his teens, yet, for the past several years, he's been shaking the rafters at pop concerts, and playing to twenty or thirty thousand screaming fans. The boy's already sold over a million albums in Great Britain, Germany, Australia, Japan, Denmark, and Norway. He's made history by being the youngest singer to have the most consecutive top ten hits in England — an accomplishment that landed him an entry in the British edition of the *Guinness Book of World Records*. He's even done something that *every* young pop singer or group can only dream of — he's been the opening act from Tokyo to Tampa for the mega-platinum group of the new millennium, Backstreet Boys.

Of course, you could say this blond-haired, brown-eyed babe had a bit of a leg up. After all, his older brother *is* Nick Carter of the Backstreet Boys. That's true, but, in spite of any cries of "nepotism," Aaron Carter has proved over and over again he's got the goods, he's got the talent and — he's got the squeal-appeal.

Music has always been in Aaron's blood. He and his twin sister, Angel, are the youngest of Bob and Jane Carter's clan of kids. Backstreet Boys' Nick is the oldest; next comes sister Bobbie Jean (or B.J.); then sister Leslie; and *then* the double blessed event of Aaron and Angel. The Florida family always had music playing around the house — and the lyrical sounds more often than not were coming from Nick's room. "I used to stand on a tree stump in our back garden and sing, pretending the flowers were my audience," Nick once told the British teen magazine *Smash Hits.*

In those days music was the background of the Carter family's life until it became front and center with a bang — when Nick joined the Backstreet Boys. Nick was thirteen years old at the time; younger brother Aaron was only five when he found himself in a front-row seat for his older brother's climb to superstardom.

The wide-eyed little boy watched it all — very carefully as Nick joined A.J. McLean, Brian Littrell,

Kevin Richardson, and Howie Dorough when BSB was just a musical project put together by Orlando, Florida, businessman Lou Pearlman. Actually most people — even those closest to Lou — thought the entire idea was a mega-money mistake. It was 1993, and the ultimate boy band phenomenon, New Kids on the Block, had already become yesterday's news. Though they had reigned high on the charts from 1989 to 1992, by 1993 the New Kids were so five-minutes-ago. The world of pop music had changed drastically.

Grunge and alternative rock and hard-core rap were dominating the airwaves, leaving the finger-snapping, feel-good tunes of such pop groups as New Kids ice cold. So, in 1993 when Lou Pearlman, a multimillion-aire who had made his fortune in the aviation business, decided to back a pop music boy band, those "in the know" just shook their heads.

What was he thinking? was the buzz around the Orlando entertainment scene. Still, the Backstreet Boys plugged on.

For over a year BSB practiced and fine-tuned their harmonies and stage show. Every day they worked hard with their voice coaches and choreographers. In what has become part and parcel of the BSB legend, the boys sweated through hours of practice in Lou's un-airconditioned airplane warehouse during the hot, humid Orlando summer. And, after close to two years of preparation, BSB released their first single, "We've Got It Goin' On."

Unfortunately, they didn't . . . at least not in the United States in 1995. The single went absolutely nowhere — it got no radio play at all! No one heard it, so no one bought it. But no one was ready to call it quits. After a lot of all-night meetings and damage-control sessions, Lou and company decided to rethink the strategy. Maybe America wasn't ready for them, but that didn't mean music loving fans in Europe weren't. The Backstreet Boys packed up and went off on their European adventure. As everyone knows, the strategy worked: BSB hit big, first in Europe, then in the United States.

All along the way, the Backstreet Boys had a number-one fan: little Aaron Carter. Aaron wasn't old enough to understand the marketing maneuvers it takes to make a platinum-selling pop group — all he knew was that his big brother was performing with his friends in front of thousands and thousands of enthusiastic fans. Soon, girls all over the world rec-ognized Nick's face wherever he went, and they all knew the lyrics to BSB songs. Aaron was incredibly proud of Nick. And Aaron began to get ideas of his own.

CHAPTER 2

Babe Alert — Aaron Carter, the Early Years

December 7, 1987 — it was time. Bob and Jane Carter quickly headed for Tampa General Hospital for an early Christmas present. Actually, you might say presents, since Jane was about to give birth to twins, Angel and Aaron Carter, at 8:01 A.M. and 8:02 A.M. Angel arrived one minute before Aaron and each weighed in at a healthy seven pounds and eleven ounces. With loud, healthy baby squalls they joined their older siblings Nick, Bobbie Jean, and Leslie as the newest members of the Carter clan.

Actually, Nick, Bobbie Jean, and Leslie were surprised by the arrival of not one, but two, additions to the family — they didn't know Jane was expecting twins. But as the babies of the family, Angel and Aaron were loved and hugged constantly. Bobbie Jean and Leslie had two little living dolls to play with and Nick, who was seven years old at the time, finally had the little brother he had hoped for. The baby boy twin had been named Aaron Charles after his grandfather, and the girl christened Angel Charissma. Soon the Carter household was once again running smoothly with its two latest members fitting right into the daily routine. And it was definitely a full schedule by the time Aaron and Angel arrived.

Music: The Family Business

When Jane and Bob Carter were first married, they lived in Jamestown, a rural town in upstate New York not far from the Pennsylvania border. Bob and his father, Aaron Carter, owned a restaurant lounge called the Yankee Rebel. Residents of Jamestown often stopped by the Yankee Rebel after work, or on the weekend for an inexpensive night on the town. There was a dance floor and when a live band wasn't playing, Bob Carter would often act as dj and spin records. Bob and Jane's eldest child, Nick, was born on January 28, 1980. Before Nick could even walk, he was a regular visitor at the Yankee Rebel. Remembering that time, Nick told *SuperTeen* magazine in one of his first Backstreet Boys interviews, "When I was real small, I used to get up there in my diapers and dance around." Today

Nick credits his love of music to those days back in Jamestown.

In 1982 Nick's sister B.J. was born, also in Jamestown. Then, in late 1984, Jane and Bob Carter decided to relocate to a warmer and sunnier climate. They moved to the Tampa, Florida, area, where they went into an entirely new business venture: the Garden Villa Retirement Home. Bob managed the residence, Jane was the chef, and Bob's mother, Barbara, helped them both. Always a good cook, Jane learned to expand her homemade recipes to make enough healthy and hearty food for the senior citizen residents *and* her own growing family.

At first the Carters actually lived at the retirement home, but soon they moved to a beautiful waterfront house in nearby Ruskin, Florida. Graced by lots of property, a refreshing and inviting in-ground pool, and a boat dock where they kept a family boat as well as several JetSkis, Jane, Bob, and the kids enjoyed every minute in their new home. They were living in this house when middle sister Leslie was born in 1986, and the twins, Aaron and Angel, in 1987. Though Aaron and Angel never actually lived at the Garden Villa Retirement Home, it was a home-away-from-home for them. Before the twins were of school age, Jane and Bob would bring them to Garden Villa every day. Because of their living arrangement, all the Carter children were brought up to be polite and considerate of the elderly. They also found they had the unique opportunity to listen and learn from the residents' personal life stories. It was a very valuable and lasting lesson for Nick, B.J., Leslie, Aaron, and Angel.

Life was good for the Carter family. The kids were healthy and happy, and the Florida lifestyle seemed to suit them perfectly. They worked and played in perfect harmony. The Tampa Bay area provided a good educational system for the kids as well as great recreational opportunities. Right in the Tampa area is Busch Gardens, one of America's largest zoological theme parks, as well as historic sites tracing the history of Florida from its very beginnings. Nearby St. Petersburg, Florida, is home to the Gulf Beaches Museum, which explores the rich history of the Tampa Bay area's barrier islands, as well as the Salvador Dalí Museum, which boasts the world's largest and most comprehensive collection of the internationally renowned Spanish artist.

Of course, within a few hours' drive of Tampa, is America's fun city: Orlando, Florida. There is something there for everyone and anyone: Walt Disney World, Sea World of Florida, and Universal Studios of Florida.

The irony is that when the Carters first moved to

Florida, they had no idea the role that entertainment opportunities available to them in their new home would play in their lives. Indeed, they soon learned that it would change *everything* for them. And it all started with Nick.

A Star Is Born

Though Nick had shown an early love of music and was never shy in front of an audience, Bob and Jane hadn't thought about a singing career for their eldest son. As with all their children, they encouraged Nick to follow his heart and his natural abilities. Nick's talents just happened to be singing and dancing. He thrived on performing. While still in grade school he began voice and dance lessons with local coaches Jane found through the Tampa Yellow Pages. While attending Frank D. Miles Elementary School, Nick appeared as Raoul, one of the lead roles, in the school production of *Phantom of the Opera*.

Oddly Nick wasn't supposed to have the role of Raoul. "I wanted to be involved in the play when the teachers first started talking about it, but I missed out," Nick revealed in *Backstreet Boys: The Official Biography* by Rob McGibbon. "Luckily, the guy who was playing the police inspector, Raoul, chickened out after a few rehearsals, so I stepped up and asked the teacher if I could do it. She asked me to sing for her. I hadn't really done that much singing before, so I was pretty shaky, but she liked my voice and I got the part.

"It was only a fun school play with a small set and props made by the teachers and some of the parents. It was nothing fancy because we were just little kids, but it was my first play ever, so it was really exciting for me. The audience was very responsive to my bits and it spurred me on. It made me think I was capable of performing and gave me a lot of confidence to do other things."

Nick not only impressed his teachers, classmates, and their families in *Phantom*, but he showed his parents that he had a special gift to be nurtured and encouraged. Over the next five years, Nick worked hard and eventually began studying with a very respected local vocal coach, Marianne Prinkey. Along with her partner Sandy Karl, Marianne worked with the Tampa Bay Buccaneers football team's cheerleaders, The Swashbucklers. It was through this connection that Nick began appearing in the NFL team's pre-game and half-time shows. At age ten, Nick performed in front of crowds of 50,000-plus. "I got such an amazing buzz when I went out on the field," Nick told biographer McGibbon. "I couldn't believe I was singing in front of so many people. One of my proudest moments was when I had to sing the national anthem before a game. There was so much pressure on me, but it was an incredible feeling to hear the cheers when I finished."

Nick Makes His Mark

Things began happening for Nick pretty quickly after that. After school, he'd routinely go out on constant rounds of auditions and tryouts. Often, he nabbed the gig. Nick landed an appearance on the national TV show, the *New Original Amateur Hour*, which he won. He also appeared in statewide commercials for the Florida State Lottery and the Money Store, and even won a small part in the Johnny Depp feature film *Edward Scissorhands*. True Nick Carter fans might recognize his blurred image as it flashes across the background of a scene in the movie. He may not have gotten his big break in *Edward Scissorhands*, but Nick *was* climbing the ladder of success one rung at a time.

However, as Nick's budding career was beginning to blossom, he wasn't finding the same appreciation at school. After Miles Elementary, Nick went to Orange Grove Middle School and then Young Junior High School. Nick never exactly understood why his classmates gave him a hard time. Perhaps it was because he often had to leave school early for auditions or because some of his classmates were jealous because he was beginning to make a showbiz name for himself. Whatever the reasons for their attitudes, Nick was made to feel like an outsider. He even remembers that some of the bigger guys tried to get him into physical fights at school. Though today Nick is 6' 1", back then he was just a little guy. "I was half the size I am now," he recalled. "So I got picked on all the time."

Even though things were rough for him, Nick continued pursuing his dreams. He may not have had a lot of friends at school, but his entire family supported every move he made — and that gave him the incentive to drive on. In 1992, when Nick was twelve years old, his big break finally came. He auditioned for a role on the Disney Channel's *New Mickey Mouse Club*. Based in Orlando at Walt Disney World, *MMC* was quickly becoming the epicenter for new, young talent. As everyone knows today, *MMC* produced such superstars as 'N Sync's Justin Timberlake and JC Chasez, *Felicity*'s Keri Russell, singers Britney Spears and Christina Aguilera, and *Remember the Titans* actor Ryan Gossling.

Nick Carter might very well have been added to that impressive list. But Nick never did become a

Mouseketeer because something else came up. At the same time Nick was singing and dancing for a set of Mouse ears, he also had auditioned for a boy band being put together by Lou Pearlman.

Lou had no real musical background, but he had played guitar in a couple of bands when he was a teenager, and now he was determined to put together a group that equaled or even outdistanced the success of the 1990s superstar boy band, New Kids on the Block.

Lou had started his search for the perfect boys and by late 1992 he had already found A.J. McLean and Howie Dorough. A.J. and Howie were two talented young singers already making a buzz on the Orlando music scene. Nick auditioned for what would eventually become the Backstreet Boys and impressed Lou with his natural talent, stage presence, and golden good looks.

According to biographer McGibbon, Lou said, "As soon as I saw Nick perform, I knew he was just what we needed. He was a cute kid with a great personality and he was really professional for his age. When he sang, he had control of the microphone and had a great voice. You could tell he was already a well-seasoned performer, even though he was just a kid."

Eventually Nick was chosen to join the group. Backstreet Boys were then rounded out by the inclusion of Kentucky cousins Brian Littrell and Kevin Richardson. It was a dream come true for Nick and the other guys, but fame and fortune were hardly handed to them on a silver platter. Backstreet Boys were not what you would call an overnight success. The early years were full of sacrifices and plenty of hard work for the boys. After more than a year of training, rehearsals, and local performances, the Backstreet Boys released their first single with Jive Records in August 1995. The song was entitled "We've Got It Goin' On" and the guys had gone over to Sweden to record the single, plus two other songs, "Nobody But You" and "Quit Playing Games (With My Heart)."

The BSB crew had high hopes for "We've Got It Goin' On," but the single only made it to the number 69 spot on *Billboard*'s pop chart. Without support from the radio stations and MTV, "We've Got It Goin' On" soon disappeared from the U.S. charts entirely. So Lou went to plan B — and in the early fall of 1995 he took BSB on their European Adventure. That was the beginning of the Backstreet Boys phenomenon.

A Family Business

Of course, one of the Backstreet Boys' earliest and most ardent fans was Nick Carter's little brother, Aaron.

After all, Aaron had seen it all from the very beginning. He learned a lot about the ups and downs of show business from his front-and-center seat for all of Nick's experiences. This up-close-and-personal view had a huge effect on the little boy — he wanted nothing more than to follow in his big brother's footsteps, and he started to do that when he was just five years old.

Aaron started kindergarten at Nick's old school, Frank D. Miles Elementary and confided to his parents that he wanted to be a singer, just like Nick. Bob and Jane sat down and had a serious talk with their youngest son. They told him they would support him in anything he wanted to do, but he had to understand that it was a long, hard road ahead . . . and success wasn't a certainty. Jane had been through it with Nick, and in her book *The Little Prince of Pop*, she recalls Aaron's first audition. "After his turn at auditioning, Aaron bounced with excitement. He felt really hopeful that he had landed the assignment. I knew the harsh reality of this business. I relied on my old clichés. The dialogue I'd had so many time before with Nick spilled out of my mouth easily.

"'Aaron,' I said, 'it doesn't matter if you get chosen for this, because the next opportunity is just waiting around the corner. If it's right, it will happen, so why worry about it? It's about having fun, honey.'"

Aaron understood — certainly a lot more than another five-year-old might have. So, even at the tender age of five, Aaron got it. He knew he had to pay his dues from the very beginning. Of course, Jane's warning speeches turned out to be unnecessary since Aaron won his first audition — a photo shoot where Aaron and an elderly model were cast as grandson and grandfather fishing together. Not only did Aaron get the job, but fishing was one of his favorite pastimes!

Modeling and appearing in ads and commercials had their appeal for Aaron, but like his older brother, his first love had always been music. As a matter of fact, it is Carter family legend that even as a toddler, little Aaron would wake up every morning singing!

"When I decided I wanted to be a singer . . . my mom encouraged me to start [my own] band," Aaron told *YT* magazine. "By the time I was seven, I was the lead singer of a group called Dead End. It was great fun."

Aaron had met three other boys at the Yamaha Rock School in Tampa, Florida, where he took singing and guitar lessons every day after his regular school classes. They formed Dead End and performed at school events and local parties. However, Dead End broke up when Aaron was nine. Besides the fact that Aaron was beginning to travel a lot with Nick and the

Backstreet Boys, he and his bandmates were having musical differences. According to the book *Backstreet Brother: Aaron Carter* by Corey Barnes, the fledgling singer revealed to British teen mag *Top of the Pops*: "I left — they wanted to do alternative music and I wanted to do more pop."

Understandably, Aaron was into pop music, it's what the Backstreet Boys were doing. But Aaron wasn't just being a copycat of his big brother — he truly loved the infectious fun of pop music. As a matter of fact, Aaron became a mini-authority on pop songs from the last four decades. He loved listening to 1960s Beach Boys songs like "Surfin' USA," Jackson Five hits of the 1970s, "Crush on You" by the 1980s group The Jets, and the 1990s mega-smashes by New Kids on the Block.

All the time he kept trying to get better at it. Aaron worked hard taking voice lessons. Nick gave him tips on improving his stage presence. His parents, the other members of BSB, the group's manager Johnny Wright, and even Lou Pearlman encouraged Aaron. As a matter of fact, Lou was so impressed with Aaron's progress that he signed him to Trans Continental Entertainment and sent him into the recording studio to make his own record. Aaron's first single was "Crush on You." The opportunity to record is one that most singers wait years for — Aaron was only nine years old.

In March 1997, Aaron got another big break: He was the "special guest" opening act for a Backstreet Boys concert in Berlin, Germany. Recalling that night, Aaron told the British teen magazine *Top of the Pops*, "They just pushed me onstage and I sang."

Of course, that wasn't exactly accurate. Aaron had a lot of confidence — after all, he'd been working long and hard on his performing skills. That night he strode onstage in front of thousands of Backstreet Boys' fans, and gave the performance of his life. As the last notes of "Crush on You" faded into the night, Aaron was greeted with a tidal wave of applause from the appreciative audience. When Aaron left the stage, his big brother and biggest fan, Nick, gave him a huge hug. It was a spectacular night — and it only got better.

Lou had arranged for an executive from Edel America Records to see the show that night, and before the evening was over, the businessmen had inked a deal for Edel to distribute Aaron's albums. Nine-year-old Aaron Carter was on his way, following in his big brother's footsteps . . . step by step!

CHAPTER 3

Oh, Brother! Nick and His Boys

When BSB arrived in Germany for the beginning of their promotional tour in 1995, they already had a fan base since "We've Got It Goin' On" was doing so well. So to give the fans more, BSB started a nonstop blitz of the country. They appeared at clubs, opened for other acts in concerts, and visited every radio station they could. They released their next single, "I'll Never Break Your Heart," and once again it proved to be a big hit in Germany. But this time, the *British* fans didn't respond as well. "I'll Never Break Your Heart" only made it to the number-42 position on the British charts. However, keeping true to their strategy, BSB continued their successful "invasion" of Germany, and also worked on new songs.

In early 1996, without even completing an album

yet, BSB released their third single, "Get Down." At last, the rest of Europe finally caught on to what the German fans had seen the year before. "Get Down" went to number 14 on the British pop chart and the Backstreet Boys were given the ultimate nod of acceptance: They were invited to appear on Britain's number-one pop music television show, *Top of the Pops* (which is like MTV's *TRL*). Backstreet Boys had finally arrived.

BSB Gets It Goin' On

In the spring of 1996, the Backstreet Boys returned home to Orlando, Florida, and finished recording the rest of their first album, *Backstreet Boys*, which they released in Europe. After they finished their studio work, BSB once again returned to Europe and undertook an exhausting tour that included countries such as Germany, England, Spain, Denmark, Norway, Sweden, and even Thailand and Korea. The sales of *Backstreet Boys* soon started hitting the platinum mark. In an interesting turnabout, it was decided to rerelease the single, "We've Got It Goin' On," and by the early fall of 1996, the single had surpassed its previous high spot on the British charts and climbed to number 3. Album sales were taking off too, and once again the boys went on a massive tour that extended to Southeast Asian markets like Hong Kong, Singapore, Japan, and Malaysia, as well as the Philippines and Australia.

Since rereleasing "We've Got It Goin' On" had worked for them, BSB rereleased "I'll Never Break Your Heart." This time it zoomed past its number 42 high spot on the British charts and reached number 8. But there was more in store for Nick, A.J., Howie, Brian, and Kevin. They had been invited to the MTV Europe Awards, and even though they were the new buzzworthy band on the scene, they felt they were too new to win any awards. However, their fans had a different idea. Through a grassroots phone-in campaign by Backstreet Boys fans, BSB won MTV Europe's "Best Group" award. That was the perfect 1996 Christmas present for the guys.

Back Home in the U.S.A.

When BSB returned to Orlando in 1997, they had only a moment or two to take a breath. By this time they had sold almost ten million copies of *Backstreet Boys* all over the world. So the plan was to record an American version of *Backstreet Boys*, which would include some reworked versions from their European debut album, as well as some entirely new songs.

Finally, America caught up to the rest of the world in noticing this group of homegrown singers. However, the Backstreet Boys knew that if they were really going to make their mark in America, they were going to have to reprise their intense performance schedule, plus undertake a massive cross-country radio promotional tour which would visit both major and smaller markets. In order to really succeed, BSB would have to meet and greet fans everywhere they went.

It would be hard work but the five guys were ready for the challenge. Even more than that, they couldn't wait to start. And they proved that they had good reason to hit the road. During 1997 and 1998, the Backstreet Boys had one major hit after another in the U.S. At one point "Quit Playing Games (With My Heart)," "As Long As You Love Me," "I'll Never Break Your Heart," "All I Have to Give" and "(Everybody) Backstreet's Back" were overlapping one another on *Billboard*'s Top 100 Singles Pop Chart!

By late winter of 1999 the Backstreet Boys had sold over twenty-eight million albums worldwide . . . and they were just getting their second wind. In May 1999, they released their second CD, *Millennium*, and sold over a million copies in the first week — a feat not beaten until 'N Sync released *No Strings Attached* in March 2000.

The singles from *Millennium* were also chart toppers. They included "Larger Than Life," "I Want It That Way," "Show Me the Meaning of Being Lonely," "It's Gotta Be You," and "I Need You Tonight." With "I Need You Tonight," BSB used a unique marketing method. Through MTV, fans voted on what the next song from *Millennium* would be, so *it was fans* who chose "I Need You Tonight" as BSB's next single. The *Millenium* album was a huge success for BSB in more than one way. Fans loved it, but also the music industry finally recognized Backstreet Boys as the talented artists they are. Instead of being dismissed as "just another pop boy band" as they were when they first came out in 1993, Backstreet Boys found themselves nominated for — and winning — MTV Awards, Grammys, and the American Music Awards. The Backstreet Boys even graced the cover of the bible of music, *Rolling Stone*, not once, but twice — the May 27, 1999, and January 20, 2000, issues.

Boys to Men

Though the Backstreet Boys released "It's Gotta Be You" and "I Need You Tonight" in the first half of 2000, they finally were able to give themselves a bit of a rest. They still made some promotional appearances on

MTV and selected concert arenas, but they decided not to go on a major tour in the spring or summer of 2000. Actually, they were busy with other things. In the late winter of 2000, it leaked out that Kevin Richardson and Brian Littrell had gotten engaged. Though at first there was a rumble of hysteria among some BSB fans, most wished the guys well. When Kevin did exchange vows with his longtime girlfriend Kristin Willits on June 18, 2000, the happy couple received thousands of telegrams, e-mails, gifts, and letters from fans all over the world.

While Kevin and Brian were working on their personal lives during this break from the Backstreet Boys, A.J. fulfilled a wild and wacky dream of his own — performing his own songs solo. Members of BSB's touring entourage were familiar with A.J.'s alter ego, singer Johnny No Name, but in March of 2000 he officially introduced the "British" artist to the public. In a mini-tour, A.J.'s bad boy, Johnny No Name, appeared in half a dozen cities across the U.S. and the proceeds went to VH1's "Save the Music" educational program. He played in smaller clubs, and sang his own songs as well as some Backstreet Boys hits. "There was lots of screaming, lots of craziness," Johnny No Name told MTV's Chris Connelly.

As for the possibility of a Johnny No Name album, A.J. told MTV's John Norris that he was considering it, but "it's not going to happen anytime before the next [Backstreet Boys] album."

And on the topic of their next album, Nick, A.J., Howie, Brian, and Kevin all admitted they were eager to get back in the studio. So, after Kevin's June wedding and a short honeymoon, the boys headed over to Sweden to once again work with producer Max Martin. Before they left, A.J. talked about BSB's third album, planned for a fall 2000 release. "We have some ideas, collectively as a group, about doing something really different for this next album that has never really been done before, which will kind of display each of our solo abilities," A.J. told John Norris of MTV.

In another MTV report shortly before they left for Sweden, Howie revealed, "We've been in the studio already, writing and doing some demos, but I think these are going to be some actual takes that we're going to do for mastering for the album. I've heard the stuff already from Sweden, and I've written a couple of things myself along with the guys. We just did a trip down to the Bahamas, where we all five wrote together for the first time as a group, and hopefully we've got a lot of great stuff that we're going to surprise everybody with."

"My music is R&B/pop," says twelve-year-old Aaron. "I've gotten more into R&B as I've gotten older."

Aaron, circa 1999. By the time he was ten years old, Aaron was already a superstar in Europe, Asia, and Australia!

Aaron's mom, Jane, is his manager. "She always gives me the best advice," he says.

If Aaron could get a tattoo, it would be either "a dragon on my back or an 'I love Mom' on my arm," confesses the young singer. Guess what — Jane says no tattoos . . . at least for now.

Aaron plays with his weimaraner, Oscar.

"At first I wanted to sing so I could be with my brother Nick," says Aaron. "Now, I just love it!"

CHAPTER 4

Backstreet Baby — Aaron's European Education

The relationship between Aaron and Nick is very special: they are buddies as well as brothers. According to Andre Csillag, the official photographer of the Backstreet Boys, "Aaron and Nick are very close. Aaron loves Nick; he thinks Nick is the most beautiful gift that he ever had. He's the biggest fan of Nick. On the other hand, Nick takes care of him with fun. They [don't] have problems together."

The closeness that Aaron and Nick share might seem a bit unusual due to the large age gap between them. Eight years is a big span, but Nick has always liked being the big brother to his siblings. And when Aaron — Nick's only brother — came along, the two boys developed a bond that would only grow with time.

For some young performers, having a little brother on the road with them might have been a hassle — but not for Nick Carter. He really enjoys having Aaron around. As a matter of fact, when the Backstreet Boys first returned to the U.S. from Europe and were off the road back home in Florida, Nick still shared a bedroom with Aaron at the Carters' house in Ruskin, Florida. "It's cool," Aaron told *Top of the Pops* magazine back then. "I wouldn't want a room of my own. . . . I think I'd be bored." Despite his success and busy schedule Nick makes time to talk to Aaron, and to share their thoughts. Recalling the time a six-year-old Aaron shared his wish to follow in his brother's footsteps and be a singer, Nick told *TeenBeat* magazine, "I definitely [saw] the urge [in] him wanting to be just as successful as I wanted to be [when I was his age]."

As for Aaron, well, he has always given Nick credit for opening the pop music door for him. "Nick has helped me so much," Aaron told *TeenBeat* magazine. "He gives me great advice and keeps me on track with my career."

The Road Show

Actually being on the road with Nick and the Backstreet Boys was an education in itself for Aaron. If you want to achieve a dream, he found out, you have to sacrifice some things. When Aaron first went onstage in

Berlin on that March night in 1997, he was making a major commitment to his future. Even though he was only nine years old at the time, Aaron realized he was given an opportunity that he had to take seriously. It wasn't all fun and games. If Aaron really wanted to have a career as a performer, he had a lot of hard work ahead of him. But Aaron was hooked by the sound of applause, and he became more determined than ever to fine-tune his talents.

At first his manager was Johnny Wright, who had worked with the Backstreet Boys during their early days and still works with 'N Sync. However, even from the start of Aaron's career, his mom Jane Carter was an intricate part of the team and she eventually took over the manager duties while Nick became Aaron's business manager. In an interview with *TeenBeat*, Aaron revealed, "Nick has helped me so much. . . . I would have never gotten a record deal if it weren't for [him] — because if Nick weren't a singer, then I wouldn't be one. He is the one who asked me if I wanted to sing. I was interested in performing before, but I think it would have been a lot harder."

The Little Prince of Pop

After his March 1997 "debut" with the Backstreet Boys, Aaron went back to square one. It was time for him to develop his own talents to the point where he could be a solo act — not just an opening act for his brother's group. So, Aaron returned to Orlando, Florida, and worked with vocal coaches and choreographers to develop his own explosive stage show. He was spending a lot of time at the Trans Continental recording studio complex (nicknamed O-Town by the press) where the Trans Con creative team worked with Aaron every day on his vocals, his choreography, and even his interview skills. Needless to say, Aaron was rubbing elbows with some pretty impressive talent at O-Town. At the time, it was the home of BSB, and 'N Sync, as well as other upcoming groups LFO, Innosence, C Note, and Take 5.

An important part of any singer's success is finding the right song. You can have the best voice, dance up a storm, and have absolutely to-die-for good looks, but if you don't have "the" song, you're *never* going to succeed. So as Aaron was working on his vocal exercises and dance routines, the powers that be at Trans Con were looking for just the right songs for Aaron.

In September 1997, Aaron was ready to return to Europe and release his first single. Everyone had decided that Aaron's first song would be "Crush on You." The song had first been popular back in the 1980s when the pop group The Jets had recorded it. Aaron, however, made "Crush on You" his very own song. It zoomed to the top of the charts in Europe and was soon joined by Aaron's second single, "Crazy Little Party Girl."

By the time Aaron celebrated his tenth birthday in December of 1997, he had released his European debut album, *Aaron Carter,* and was on his way to becoming the youngest pop star in Europe. In 1998, Aaron released several more singles from his album — the ballad "I'm Gonna Miss You Forever" and the bouncy pop anthem "Shake It." All his songs were so popular that he was actually giving the Backstreet Boys some competition on the European charts! As a matter of fact, Aaron received an honor not even big brother Nick did — Aaron was added to the 1998 British Edition of *Guinness Book of World Records* for being the youngest singer to have the most consecutive top ten hits! Aaron soon began adding to the Carter family's collection of gold and platinum albums. *Aaron Carter* was released in Canada in January of 1998 and was a huge success. By the time the album was released in the United States in 1998, it had already gone either gold or platinum in England, Spain, Norway, Canada, and Germany!

As Aaron embarked on his own mini-tour in the summer of 1998, he claims he always kept something Nick told him in mind. In an interview with the *Toronto Sun* newspaper, Aaron said, "He told me, 'Watch out for the fans. The fans are so nice and you should respect your fans. Meet them and sign [autographs] for them because they buy your albums.'" It's a piece of advice that Aaron has never forgotten.

Even the adults who worked with Aaron saw him grow into a savvy, dedicated performer. "Nothing can stop Aaron, he's unbelievable," a record label spokesperson said. "He has so much confidence, and such a love of performing. I don't know if I've ever seen anyone who gets more pleasure out of getting onstage and just doing everything in his power to try and put a smile on people's faces."

And people everywhere *are* smiling. In 1999, Aaron joined superstar artists 98°, No Authority, Tatyana Ali, and EYC for Nickelodeon's "All That Music & More" tour. From the reviews, you would have thought Aaron owned the entire show.

In the *Pittsburgh Post Gazette*, the reviewer wrote, "Backstreet Boy Nick Carter's little brother Aaron turned in a winning performance that couldn't have been more adorable, stopping a song with the chorus, 'Everybody get wild' to tell the boys and girls:

'While you're out there getting wild, remember . . . we are the future.' Aaron's smile-inducing set was no doubt helped along by the fact that he's only eleven, incredibly tiny and blond, with a heartbreaker's smile and sound that's cuter and more personality-driven than Nick's group."

That review wasn't a one-time rave. During the same concert tour, the *Huntsville Times* music critic checked out Aaron and the other acts when they appeared at the Von Braun Center. Aaron's time onstage seemed to stop the show. "Aaron Carter, eleven-year-old hit sensation (and little bro to Backstreet Boy, Nick Carter) was the first act, opening with 'Getting Wild,' as he rolled onstage on a scooter. [He may be small, but] Aaron doesn't let his little size interfere with his singing talents. He has a great voice. . . ."

And that was a fact that millions and millions of fans all over the world agreed with!

CHAPTER 5

Jivin' . . . Back in the U.S.A.

"Work as hard as you can. That's what I always did" — this is another piece of advice Nick gave Aaron very early in the "young prince's" career. It is a lesson Aaron learned well. And it was a lesson Aaron had to learn on his own, without big brother Nick there to guide him every step of the way.

In 1999 the Carters bought a beautiful ranch in southern California. Nick, however, kept his official address in the Tampa Bay area of Florida where he bought his own house. Of course, Nick was hardly ever there because the Backstreet Boys were too busy recording, and releasing their album *Millennium*. Before Nick could even try to settle in his new digs, BSB was off touring in support of the album. However, the end result was still the same: For the first time in Aaron's life he didn't share a bedroom with big brother

Nick! In the Carters' California home, Aaron had his own room. Of course, Aaron would be the first to say that though there is something to be said about having a whole room to yourself, he did miss having Nick around a lot. Aaron even missed Nick's snoring!

The Beat Goes On

But Aaron didn't have too much time to concentrate on what wasn't there — it was time for Aaron to make some major decisions and take some big steps forward professionally. The first move was for him to sign a recording contract with Jive Records, which of course just happens to be the Backstreet Boys' label. That took place in late 1999. The next move was to get to work on his new album. Aaron spent the early part of the new millennium in the studio recording *Aaron's Party (Come Get It)*. With eleven songs and a bunch of "conversations" with Aaron's friends about getting to-gether peppered between them, the CD really does make you feel as if you've been invited to a party with Aaron Carter.

Once Aaron put the finishing recording studio touches on *Aaron's Party (Come Get It)*, he barely had time to take a deep breath before heading into one of the most important times for a recording artist: the publicity blitz. That means letting people know about the album. Aaron spent most of the spring of 2000 crisscrossing the country making personal appearances, visiting radio stations, and doing interviews with magazines and online chats. He also spent a lot of time doing photo shoots — after all, everyone wanted to see the "new" Aaron Carter. Many people think of Aaron as the mop-haired cutie who first appeared with the Backstreet Boys. The "new" Aaron has shorter, spiky hair — definitely a cooler look.

By June 2000, Aaron was coming into the final stretch. He and his mom headed up to Toronto, Canada. But it wasn't a vacation trip for them — it was all work. In a matter of a couple of weeks, Aaron made five different videos for songs from his upcoming album. And that was just the beginning. From July 31, 2000, to August 14, 2000, he joined Britney Spears' sold-out summer tour for eleven different concert appearances — from Los Angeles, California, to Salt Lake City, Utah.

On August 1, 2000, "Aaron's Party (Come Get It)" was released as the first single from the CD with the same name. Aaron spent his off-tour time making a multitude of TV appearances — Nickelodeon's *Snick House* on August twelfth, *The Fox Teen Choice*

Awards on August twenty-second, and Fox Family's *HiFi Room* on September twenty-third. Finally, on September 26, 2000, the CD, *Aaron's Party (Come Get It)* was released. By then Aaron Carter had definitely earned the title, Little Prince of Pop!

CHAPTER 6

Aaron Carter's Complete Checklist

Personal Info

Full Name: Aaron Charles Carter (Aaron was named after his Grandfather)

Nicknames: "Little Prince of Pop" — Aaron's European record company, Edel, gave him this nickname. He's also been dubbed "Big A" by one of his producers, "AC" by the Backstreet Boys, and "Airboy" by friends. (Some very close family members used to call him "Chuckie," which was also his grandfather's nickname.)

Birthdate: December 7, 1987

Astro Sign: Sagittarius

Birthplace: Tampa, Florida

Birth Hospital: Tampa General Hospital

Current Residence: Marina Del Ray, California

Height: 5'2" — and growing!

Weight: 90 pounds

Hair: Blond

Eyes: Brown

Righty or Lefty: Aaron is right-handed

Parents: Robert (Bob) Gene and Jane Spaulding Carter

Siblings: Nick Gene (20), Bobbie Jean (18), Leslie Barbara (14), and twin sister Angel Charissma (12). Aaron also has a half sister, Ginger, from his dad's first marriage.

Grandparents: Jane's parents, Helen Neal and Doug Spaulding — Doug Spaulding is now married to Linda Spaulding. Bob's parents, Barbara "Barb" Carter and Aaron Charles "Chuck" Carter.

Uncles: Jane's brothers Scott, Steve, and John Spaulding

Cousins: John, Arynn, Stephen, Adam, Joshua, and Alexander Spaulding (Steve and Debbie Spaulding's children); Dustin and Derek Spaulding (Scott and Roxanne Spaulding's children); Scott Spaulding (John and Denise Spaulding's son)

Best Friend: Paul Webster

Tutor: Mary

Pets: Aaron has two dogs — a weimaraner named Oscar, and a golden retriever named Simba. There are eleven more family dogs, including two rottweilers named Pharaoh and Sky; a Siberian husky named JoJo; two mini-schnauzers named Salt and Pepper (though they now live with Aaron's grandmother Barbara); a German shepherd named Samson; a shih tzu named Merlin (this is B.J.'s dog); a pug; and three others. They also have three birds — a white cockatoo; a blue parakeet; and a green tropical; a lizard named Babyface; and two cats named Bandit and Lucky.

Collections: Hats, Beanie Babies (his favorites are, according to his mom, Bronty Brontosaurus, the dinosaur; Razor, the red wild boar; Flutter, the butterfly; Bumble, the bumblebee; Garcia, the tie-dyed bear; and Crunch, the shark), Pokémon cards, and motorcycles (even though Aaron isn't old enough to have a driver's license, he can ride his motorcycles and dirt bikes on his family's property and during supervised outings on the trails in the Mojave Desert)

Hobbies: Making model cars, which he has lined up in his room. His favorites are a red Ferrari and a black Mercedes convertible that he proudly says, "I put it all together myself — it's not from a kit."

Vehicles: Two bicycles, a motor scooter, a dune buggy, JetSkis, skateboards, a dirt bike, and two motorcycles — a white Honda XR80 and a Kawasaki KX80

Instruments: Saxophone, drums, piano, and guitar

Fears: Spiders ("ickkkkkk!") and sharks

"Best" Body Part: "My hair" — Aaron revealed this fact in an online interview: "It takes about three minutes to do my hair because all I have to do is brush it and put some gel in it and mess it all up on the top. Pretty easy, huh?"

"Worst" Body Part: "My feet" — Aaron gives no explanation why he doesn't like his feet (we think they're pretty cute!).

Shoe Size: 7

Role Model: His brother Nick

Prized Possessions: Aaron keeps his treasures in a small jewelry box in his bedroom. According to *TeenBeat* magazine, they include "objects he has found around the world — pennies, a folded piece of green paper with the names of the dancers he tours with, a silver dollar his father gave him, half a heart he shares with a friend, and a black glass cross." Aaron told *Bop* magazine that the seventeen pennies he has in the box were also given to him by his dad. "[He] had them from a long time ago," Aaron explained. "I don't want to ruin them."

Phobia: "I'm claustrophobic," Aaron told *TeenBeat* magazine. "Very. When we were in the bus in Germany, there was a bunk called the captain bunk and it's really small, with room for one person. I'd go in there and sleep sometimes. I'd be cramped up there in the back, and [as a joke] Nick would start stuffing pillows in there. He'd be stuffing them and stuffing them and I'd be, like, [pounding to get out]!"

Worst Habit: "Biting my fingernails."

Least Fave Household Chore: "Taking the garbage out — I even got cut doing that and had to get butterfly stitches," Aaron revealed in a Zoog Disney interview.

Little-Known Fact: Aaron was in the 1997 movie *Blackrock*. He played the role of a surfer.

Biggest Turnoff: Wearing dirty clothes!

Secret Dream: "I want to be an actor and win an Oscar!"

Surprising Fact: Aaron still has his baby blanket — but it's in storage.

Animal Fantasy: "If I were an animal, I'd want to be a cat so I could climb everywhere."

Childhood Faves

Memory: "When my brother [Nick] played director and we made movies."

Cherished Possession: A Mickey Mantle autographed rookie baseball card given to him by his grandfather

Family Tradition: Boating
Water Memory: Aaron once caught a nine-inch shark.
Scariest TV Show: *Tales of the Crypt*
Board Game: Monopoly
Book: R.L. Stine's *Goosebumps* series
Candy: M&M's with peanuts
Sport: Skateboarding
Spice Girl: Posh Spice, Victoria
Video Game: James Bond
Cars: Lamborghini, Porsche, and BMW
Ice Cream: Chocolate
TV Shows: *The Wonder Years* and *Full House*
Movies: *Jurassic Park* and *Teenage Mutant Ninja Turtles 1–3* ("My favorite Turtle is Michelangelo.")
Collections: Model dinosaurs — he had more than thirty; Ninja Turtles; Tamagotchis
Nick Joke: "Nick tells me a joke like, 'Hey, Aaron! You know what I like best about you? Nothing!'" Aaron laughingly recalled in an online interview.
Halloween Costume: "The pumpkin [costume] that my mom made because I could stick my arms in and hide inside of it," Aaron said in a press conference.

Faves These Days
Colors: Blue and green
Chewing Gum: Bubblicious

45

Drink: Blue Gatorade

Soda: Sprite and Pepsi

Candy: Jolly Rancher lollipops and Twix (Aaron throws the Jolly Ranchers from the stage to his fans when he performs "Sugar, Sugar.")

Chocolate Bar: Milky Way

After-school Snack: Fruit Rollups

Ice Cream: Egg nog (But Aaron has to stay away from ice cream because he's actually allergic to it! In an online chat, Aaron revealed, "I'm allergic to dairy products, so I can only eat sherbert.")

Sandwich: Bacon, lettuce, and tomato sandwich

Aaron's Special Sandwich Creation: Pretzels, hot dog, pickles, mayonnaise, and lettuce

Fast Food Restaurant: McDonald's — "I can eat two Big Macs and fries!"

Refrigerator Raid: Milk and cookies

Breakfast: Count Chocula cereal

Lunch: Pizza or chicken with cream of mushroom soup

Dinner: Sushi, lasagna, spaghetti, or steak

Desert: Banana cream pie

Sports: Motocross, baseball, swimming, surfing, fishing, and football (Aaron played in a Little League football team as quarterback.)

Sports Teams: Baseball — Oakland Athletics; football — Tampa Bay Buccaneers

Athlete: John Elway, the former quarterback for the NFL's Denver Broncos

Animals: Tigers and wolves

Motorcycle: Kawasaki KX80-Two stoke/6 speed

Cars: Viper and Hummer

Number: Seven

Cartoon Show: *Johnny Bravo* on the Cartoon Network

TV Shows: *Friends, Seinfeld* reruns

All-Time Movie: *Stand By Me*

Actors: Sylvester Stallone and Arnold Schwarzenegger

Actresses: Sandra Bullock, Angelina Jolie, and Julia Roberts

Rock Band: Metallica

Pop Bands: Backstreet Boys and 'N Sync

Rap Artists: DMX and Dr. Dre

Female Singers: Jessica Simpson, Monica, and Mariah Carey

Country Singers: Shania Twain and Garth Brooks

Backstreet Boys Song: "As Long As You Love Me"

Comedian: Chris Rock

Books: *Robin Hood, The Complete Dog Book for Kids* (Aaron's Mom bought him this one when they got his weimaraner, Oscar)

Author: J.K. Rowling — the *Harry Potter* series

Clothing Designer: Tommy Hilfiger

Style of Clothes: "Casual stuff, sportswear, like khakis"

Clothing Store: Roots

Boxers or Briefs: Boxers

Sports Shoe: Nike — "They are the most comfortable and better for sports."

Historical Era: The 1960s — "because of the Hippies"

Ride at Disney World: Tower of Terror

State in the U.S.A.: Florida

Vacation Place: Hawaii

Hobbies: Videogames and fly-fishing

Video Game Platforms: Nintendo, Sony PlayStation

Video Game: *Spyro the Dragon*

Holidays: December seventh — his birthday; Christmas

Gift from Nick: "The best one was a toy panther," Aaron told *BOP* magazine. "It's bigger than me and [when Nick brought it back from his tour] it nearly didn't fit on the plane!"

Piece of Jewelry: A ring given to him by a friend — "I really don't take it off. It brings me good luck."

Type of Girl: "I like a girl who is a lot of fun," Aaron told *TeenBeat* magazine. "It doesn't really matter what she looks like."

Perfect Date: Britney Spears

Expression: "Hey" — Aaron uses it as a way of saying "Hello, how are you?"

Aaron's Personal Video Views

Dragonheart: "This was a really good movie. I liked the dragon because he said cool things and breathed fire over everyone. There was also a really cool fight scene at the end."

The Lion King: "I love this movie because it makes me laugh and then I feel really sad when the [father lion] dies."

Beauty and the Beast: "I like films which can scare you but make you happy too. I like the Beast in it — he really made me think he was a monster until you found out he wasn't."

Bean: "It was kinda cool. [Bean] is really kinda stupid — isn't he? He made me laugh because he pulled stupid faces and did all these things that were so dumb that you wanted to laugh the whole time."

School Stuff

Best Subjects: Science and music

Worst Subject: Math — that's what Aaron told Scholastic magazines, but in some interviews he says it's his favorite subject!

Grade School: Ruskin Elementary School, Ruskin, Florida

Foreign Language: "I'm studying German." And Aaron also speaks a little bit of French, Italian, and Japanese.

Fave Short Story He Read for School: "It was one by Edgar Allan Poe — he writes scary stories. It was a pretty old one of his. It was called 'The Werewolf House' or something like that. And it was so scary. Every night before I went to bed, I'd look around my room and under my bed, and I'd close all my curtains. I'd always keep a baseball bat by my bed because I was so scared. It was really good!"

Fave Teacher: Mrs. Matthews, Aaron's fifth-grade English teacher

Fantastic Firsts

Concert: Janet Jackson

CD Bought: *Ninja Turtles*

Concert Where He Performed: A Backstreet Boys concert in Berlin, Germany — Aaron was one of the opening acts

Book Read: *The Caterpillar Book*

Theme Park: Disney World

Movie: *Land Before Time*

What He Notices About a Girl: "Her eyes — I like girls with pretty eyes."

Body Piercing: Aaron got his left ear pierced in December 1999.

Date: Not yet — Aaron can't date until he is fifteen!

CHAPTER 7

Aaron's Funtastic Profile

Aaron Carter: The Write Stuff
His Quickie Handwriting Analysis

Though the art of handwriting analysis may not be as scientific as DNA tests or even psychological tests, it certainly is a fun way of figuring out someone's personality traits. *PopPeople* checked out Aaron's pen-to-paper offerings and came up with a thumbnail sketch of the Little Prince of Pop's inner secrets.

Aaron Carter

    Aaron signs his autograph in several different ways, but the "A" of Aaron and the "C" of Carter are always larger than the rest of the letters of his name. According to handwriting analysts, that means he has a warm and outgoing personality, that he makes friends wherever he goes.

The smaller size of the lowercase letters in his name indicates that Aaron is capable of intense concentration.

The upward slant of his signature reveals a positive outlook on life.

Underlining his name shows that Aaron is a natural leader.

The T-bar in Carter is crossed mainly on the right-hand side; according to some handwriting analysts, this means that Aaron does not put things off until later, that he deals with a job or a problem right away.

Numerology

Aaron's Personal Digits Reveal What Makes Him Tick

Personality Number — He's Number One!
This number reveals your attitude and approach to life. It is determined by separately adding the numbers of your birthday and your birth month until you have a single digit for each. Then add the two totals until it is a single digit.

Aaron's birth month is December and his birthday is 7:

1. December = 12, the twelfth month.
2. Add the numbers to find a single digit: $1 + 2 = 3$. So, the month number is 3.
3. Birth day = 7, the seventh day.
4. Add month number and birth day:

$$3 + 7 = 10$$
$$1 + 0 = 1$$

Aaron's Personality Number is 1. This indicates that he is determined and single-minded and likes to have his own way. Sometimes this trait can lead to being a bit stubborn, so it is something Aaron might want to watch out for.

What's Your Number?

Figure it out and see if you really match these other personality traits.

2: Friendly, easy to get along with, good-natured, compassionate, and sensitive. A good listener.

3: Complex and changing — you can be the bashful baby one day and the superstar the next day.

4: Loyalty is the key word here. Also dependable and dedicated to whatever you are trying to accomplish.

5: On the go, always active and stimulated by your surroundings. You want to know everything, go everywhere, and experience new things all the time.

6: Team leader is the best definition for this number. You get along with people and are very responsible.

7: You may be called a bit of a loner. You often prefer to be by yourself or with just your closest friend. You love to read and study.

8: Strength is your main trait. You are determined to be the one people listen to and follow. You back it up with being the best you can be whether it is as a student, a friend, or athlete.

9: Like number 3, you are changeable. Sometimes you are totally by the rule and other times you are a rebel. Be careful of your temper!

Love-Scope

What the Stars Say About Aaron the Romantic

Aaron was born on December 7, 1987. His astrological sign is Sagittarius (November 22–December 21), which is a Fire Sign. That can make for some pretty exciting relationships!

The sign of Sagittarius contains an arrow, much like Cupid's telltale icon. Those born under the sign of Sagittarius are often very outgoing and social. They love going out, but often like to play the field rather than settle down with just one particular someone. Honesty in all relationships is of utmost importance to those born under this sign. They do not like playing games, and are completely up front about their feelings and commitments. However, when a Sagittarius does fall in love, it is total and complete. They may not send frilly little valentines and write love poems, but they will always be there for their true love.

Dream Date for Aaron: Miss Right for Aaron Carter must be a girl who shares his adventurous spirit, and his spur-of-the-moment sensibility. According to most astrologers, the complementary love signs for a Sagittarius are Libra and Gemini for fun, fun, fun relationships that are usually not too long-term. For long-lasting romances, those born under Sagittarius often find true love with those ruled by Leo.

Scream Date for Aaron: The sign to avoid at all cost is Virgo — they tend to be way too controlled for the fun-loving Sagittarius!

Astro-File

Spotlight on the Sagittarius

Sagittarius guys often are best friends with Gemini girls. They are best in the role of big brother/guy next door. They'll encourage you to follow your dreams, and even give you dating tips!

Those under the sign of Sagittarius are usually imaginative, sensitive, enthusiastic, optimistic, and total individualists. However, they should watch out for tendencies toward being nervous and withdrawn and making promises they can't keep.

Sagittarius' element is Fire, but it can be Hot Fire or Cool Fire. Since Aaron was born on December seventh he is ruled by Hot Fire.

Top jobs for Sagittarius: Globetrotting news reporter, scientist, explorer, pilot, politician, or headlining entertainer.

Best Friend Signs: Libra, Aquarius, and Aries

The planet Neptune rules those born under Sagittarius. They tend to have a strong sense of fair play and right and wrong.

Ruled By the Number 7 (Aaron's fave number!)

Lucky Day: Thursday

Lucky Animal: Dog

Also born on December seventh: NBA superstar player and coach Larry Bird; legendary singer and creator of the charity World Hunger Year, Harry Chapin; actor Eli Wallach; and writer Willa Cather.

The 411 On Aaron's Name

As in Numerology, you can find out personality traits by your Name Number. To determine the specific number, set up a grid:

1	2	3	4	5	6	7	8	9
A	B	C	D	E	F	G	H	I
J	K	L	M	N	O	P	Q	R
S	T	U	V	W	X	Y	Z	

Find the number that matches the letters of your first name. For Aaron it would be:

A A R O N
1 1 9 6 5

Add the numbers together until you have a single-digit number. For Aaron it would be:

$$1 + 1 + 9 + 6 + 5 = 22$$
$$2 + 2 = 4$$

The number for Aaron is 4.

The number 4 represents those who are logical, loyal, and super learners. They love to discuss almost any topic, and often get into debates. Sometimes, their tendency to challenge may hurt feelings, so they should try to be a bit more diplomatic.

What does your name-number mean? Check it out!

1: You are a leader, very imaginative, self-confident, and determined. You like being number one.

2: You are the complete people person — you love being in the mix of things, keeping things fun and happy. You're a jokester . . . and you love to go out dancing!

3: You could hold public office. You definitely can communicate your ideas to others. You're very imaginative and charming . . . in both speech and style.

4: See Aaron's profile.

5: You could be a battery charger — you have more energy than ten people put together! You think quick on your feet and love to experience new people and places.

6: Though some might think you a bit conservative, your honesty and straightforward approach to life makes you one of the most popular people in your group.

7: Something of a loner, you like to think about things and analyze them before you act. Just be careful you don't miss out on experiencing life by thinking about it too much!

8: Dream on! You are organized, self-confident, and have a definite set of goals. You dream of making the world a better place to live, and with your self-assured approach to life, you will!

9: Sensitive is the word for you. You treat people the way you like to be treated. You are very aware of others' feelings, and often people seek you out for your advice.

CHAPTER 8

Aaron Answers 53 Serious 'n' Silly Questions

The following pages include some of the most often asked questions about the Little Prince of Pop, Aaron Carter . . . as well as some little-known answers.

1. Does Aaron Carter have any tattoos?

A: No, not at this time, but during an Internet chat in April 2000 Aaron did tell a fan that if he got any tattoos he would get "a dragon on my back and an 'I Love Mom' on my left arm . . . and a mean-looking smiley face on my forearm."

2. How does Aaron spend his off hours?

A: Lots of different ways, but mostly it seems he likes to ride his motorcycles. "I got a new motorcycle for my last birthday," Aaron told *SuperTeen* magazine. "It's about thirteen inches bigger than my last one and a lot faster! I love to just go, just ride it. Where I live [in California] it's actually common [to ride motorcycles]. People actually race their bikes for a living. They'll take them and jump them over hills and stuff. I have a hill about fifteen feet [high], and sometimes I take my motorcycle and jump over it. The highest I've gone is forty-something feet on my bike."

3. Does Aaron have a girlfriend?

A: Not at the moment, but back in March 1998, Aaron admitted to the British teen magazine *BIG!* that he did have a special girl. "Her name was Jackie. We're not together anymore, but I still really like her. I met her on the set of the video for 'Shake It.' She starred in it because I liked her so much. She didn't like me very much at first — she thought I was a bit goofy, but then we got to be friends. . . . We [broke up] because we couldn't find time to see each other. She lives in Kissimmee, Florida, and I live in Tampa and that's about three hours away by car. She sent me a letter [recently] and I sent her a tape of my album, but she's at school and I'm always away."

4. Is Aaron's twin sister Angel jealous of his success?

A: No way! Aaron explained to a Dutch teen magazine called *Hitkrant*, "Angel is not at all jealous of me. She is more like a model. She doesn't want to be onstage. She has more of an interest in girl stuff — clothes, makeup, and that stuff. Angel and I have a special relationship. She is with me at my concerts and I like that. [With her there], it [feels] like I'm home."

Aaron also told *Top of the Pops Magazine*, "Everyone [in my family is] doing his or her own thing. My twin sister Angel is going to try modeling and my older sister Bobbie isn't really into music. Leslie, my other sisters, wants to sing and she might be doing backing vocals on my next single."

5. Does Aaron believe in aliens from outer space?

A: Aaron did tell the British teen magazine *Smash Hits*, "Yes, I do [believe in aliens]. Sometimes, driving back from Orlando, we see [what could be] little UFOs, like bright lights that flash. They're here, then they disappear, and then — whoosh! — they're here again! I reckon they're trying to catch someone . . . and having fun." When the magazine interviewer asked Aaron what he would look like if he were an alien, Aaron answered, "I'd have three faces! One face would pop open, then another face would come out, and then a little face would come out of my mouth! The little face would have two big bulging eyes, and its eyelashes would point out really sharp — sharper than anything in the world! And his teeth would be about three inches long. I'd be a horrible alien, scaring everyone with my teeth!"

6. Who's neater — Aaron or Nick?

A: No question here. "I'm very neat, but Nick's really messy," claimed Aaron in a magazine article. "His stuff is all over the place and I end up picking it up."

7. When Aaron was a little boy, did he make up stories?

A: Well, according to a chat Aaron had with Scholastic magazines, the answer is a resounding YES! "Oh, yeah. I used to make up [tons of stories] . . . I used to be the biggest storyteller around," Aaron laughed. "Stories about alligators and stuff like that. So many stories . . . it was unbelievable!"

8. How would Aaron like to decorate his bedroom?

A: "I'd love to make my bedroom like a jungle room," Aaron told *SuperTeen*. "It would have rocks and stuff. Have you ever seen the [restaurant] the Rainforest Café? It would look like that, with big animals moving everywhere. And branches — I'd be like Tarzan swinging all over!"

9. Aaron's family has thirteen dogs — where do they all sleep?

A: Well, there is a lot of space at the Carter family's new California ranch, but according to Aaron, "Anywhere they want!"

10. What's the weirdest thing Aaron would order as topping for a pizza?

A: "Oysters and anchovies," Aaron revealed. "I love oysters! I like sardines, too."

11. Is there anything Aaron would never leave his house without?

A: "My Sony PlayStation," he told *Tigerbeat*.

12. What is Aaron's favorite subject in school?

A: "I don't really have a favorite subject," he admitted. "But if I was to pick, it would probably be English."

13: What would fans be surprised to know about the Carters' new California ranch?

A: Aaron revealed in *16* magazine that the ranch is so far out in the country that sometimes coyotes come around. "My dog Oscar comes in the house once in a while," Aaron explained. "He sleeps with me in my room and he protects me because sometimes I'll hear coyotes scratching on my windows."

Aaron also discussed Oscar with another magazine. "He's a really good dog and he protects me at night when I'm sleeping. He'll sleep on the bed with me. It's really funny because it's almost like a human soul is in him. He'll sleep on me, and he'll crawl under the covers and swerve way up and I'll give him a pillow to lay on. . . . He'll come

65

up to me and jump over me and kind of give me a hug almost."

And in Jane Carter's book on Aaron, *The Little Prince of Pop*, the young singer recalled, "Oscar grew pretty fast. He loves to sleep on my bed with me. That's become a bit of a problem. He's so big. One night he sprawled across my bed, and there was no room for me. So I finally just got out of bed, piled up my blankets on the floor, and went to sleep."

14. Would Aaron ever date a fan?

A: "Um, well, I'm not allowed to date anyone right now," Aaron told *Shout* magazine. "But one day I want to have five girlfriends, no wait, ten. No, actually twelve!"

15. Does Aaron have a recording studio at his family's California ranch?

A: Yes. It's located right between the main house and a converted guest house. Not only does it have state-of-the-art recording equipment, but it also has a full rehearsal area with a wooden dance floor and full length mirrors so he can practice his moves. "I spend a lot of time in there," Aaron told a visiting reporter.

16. Where does Aaron keep his collection of Beanie Babies?

A: "They are in a cabinet at the foot of my bed," Aaron described to an interviewer. "It's so full I can't fit any more in it!" (According to his mom, Aaron has over three hundred Beanie Babies! — no wonder they don't fit in the cabinet!)

17. What does Aaron consider the worst thing about being a pop star?

A: "Traveling all the time," he told *Bop* magazine. "I have to go through airports, and you've got to make it on time for flights!"

18. Which member of the Backstreet Boys does Aaron consider the "craziest"?

A: "A.J. — he's really crazy," Aaron told *TV Hits* magazine. "He, like, walks around going 'Mmmmblllrrb' [Aaron makes strange mumbling noises] and pulling all these weird kinda faces. And . . . he always wears sunglasses — even indoors. But he's really good fun, too."

19. How did Aaron celebrate his first hit record, "Crush on You"?

A: Aaron told *Top of the Pops Magazine,* "I was in London. I went out to a restaurant with some of my friends and met fans who had bought my record. I usually have to be in bed by ten P.M., but this time I stayed up all night — that was because I was leaving the hotel at five in the morning, so there was no point sleeping."

20. Since Aaron grew up in Florida and now lives in California, he must like to swim. Is he a good swimmer?

A: "I'm a really strong swimmer," Aaron told *Live & Kicking* magazine. "The backstroke is my favorite so I can look up and around and see what's going on because my face isn't in the water."

21. What's the scariest thing that has ever happened to Aaron?

A: "Well, I can remember when I was a baby . . . I [almost] died," Aaron told British teen magazine *BIG!* "I did. I [almost] died! I drowned in the pool! I was two and my dad found me. I was ten seconds away from dying. I jumped in the water as I was walking past the pool and sank like a stone. [My dad saved me.] He gave me the kiss of life. I was lucky. I could have been killed."

Aaron's mom, Jane, recounted the incident in more detail to *TeenBeat* magazine. "[Aaron was] about one and a half. [He] just started to walk. . . . The pool was attached to a room that had a sliding glass door with a pin in it, and one of the older kids pulled the pin out of the door and left the door open. Bob was in the garage, and I was at work. . . . [Bob] did CPR on [Aaron] and luckily got him breathing. Thank God he knew CPR, because by the time the ambulance got there, [it would have been too late]."

22. If Aaron could be a planet in our solar system, which one would he be?

A: Believe it or not, Aaron was asked this question in a British online questionnaire. He answered simply, "Saturn, because it looks cool with its rings around it."

23. If Aaron weren't a singer, what career would he pursue?

A: Though Aaron loves the life of a pop star, he has other future plans too. In an online chat, he said, "I am going to go to college to be a marine biologist because I am obsessed with water life. I like being around the ocean. I've lived near the ocean all my life."

24. Does Aaron have a favorite dream he'll never forget?

A: Yes. "I dreamt that I was swimming with dolphins and nice sharks in the sea," Aaron told *TV Hits* magazine.

25. Has Aaron ever caused a "rock star" problem when he was staying in a hotel?

A: Well, Aaron confessed to *Top of the Pops Magazine* that he did go a little wild once. "I had the music up really loud in a hotel room in Madrid. The people next door called the desk and complained. I was listening to Metallica while jumping around on the bed, and when the guy came and knocked on the door I hid. I let my mom take care of it. . . .

Where did I hide? I lifted the TV out of the cabinet and crawled in there!"

26. If Aaron could choose any member of the Backstreet Boys other than Nick as a brother, who would it be?

A: "I guess it would be Brian, because he's the one I hang out with the most," Aaron said in an interview. "But nobody could be a better brother than Nick."

27. When Aaron was on the road with the Backstreet Boys, did they play practical jokes on each other?

A: You bet! "One time, I hid A.J.'s jacket and another time the boys locked me in my dressing room," Aaron told *Shout* magazine. "My mom was outside going, 'Give me the key, A.J.' But they kept me locked in there for ages!"

In an interview with *BIG!,* Aaron revealed, "Nick and Brian — they have so many practical jokes up their sleeves! Nick [offered me a piece of gum], and when I [tried to pull it out], it snapped my finger! [Another time Nick] put sneezing powder on my shoulder and I was sneezing all day."

Aaron also recalled the time when the Backstreet Boys "treated me like a little brother. One time they put toothpaste in my ears, and it's hard to get out! I had to wash and scrub my ears!"

28. Has Aaron ever had a crush on a celebrity?

A: Aaron confessed he did. "Neve Campbell and Jennifer Love Hewitt," he said. "And for girls my age, Mary-Kate and Ashley Olsen."

29. Is there anything Aaron would like to change to make the world a better place?

A: Aaron told *Smash Hits* magazine, "Sickness is what I'd like to change. If I ever made enough money, I'd give it to every single charity."

30. Does Aaron surf?

A: In an interview with *Live & Kicking* magazine, Aaron revealed, "Of course I can surf and I love to hang out on the beach all the time. [The biggest wave I rode] was twelve feet high — it was much taller than me, but I still surfed it. I wasn't scared at all. I got caught by a few waves and went under [a couple of times] — that feels like being in a washing machine. I swallowed lots of water."

31. Does Nick share Aaron's love of motorcycles?

A: Uh, not according to Aaron. In a chat with *SuperTeen* magazine, Aaron laughed. "My dad and I . . . we're the only people in the family who are gutsy. Nick's a chicken actually. He is. He doesn't like motorcycles or anything like that. The first time he rode a motorcycle he was so nervous, he let out the clutch too fast and he popped a wheelie. He was like 'Uuuhhaaaah!' and then he had to crash down and he went flying off. It was actually quite funny."

32. What was the biggest obstacle Aaron had to overcome to be a performer?

A: In an interview with Scholastic magazines shortly before *Aaron's Party (Come Get It)* was released, Aaron confessed, "Well, a long time ago when I was in school, I used to be very shy. When [the teachers] would call on me, I'd be really shy and I'd talk [very low]. My voice would be [really] quiet. One of my teachers, Mrs. Matthews, helped me. She'd keep me after school and talk to me. She told me not to be so scared."

33. If Aaron could go back in time to a different period in history, which one would he pick?

A: In his Scholastic interview, Aaron chose the 1950s. "I'd like to be a little boy in the 1950s, so I could grow up to invent Yahoo and make millions of [dollars]! I would be the next Bill Gates!"

34. Aaron used to have long hair. Does he like it now that he's cut it much shorter?

A: "I had a lot of hair — too much hair," Aaron laughed in an interview with *SuperTeen*. "[When I got it cut], it felt good. When I woke up in the morning, it was still in the same place. There weren't pieces of hair stickin' [up] everywhere. [The only thing I miss is] when I had it long, my sister used to make Mohawks. It was really funny."

35. What is the best piece of advice Nick ever gave Aaron?

A: Aaron told Scholastic magazines, "To stay away from drugs. That's what he told me — he told me to stay away from drugs and alcohol because that's what he's done all his life. I'm never going to do it."

36. Is it true that a snake bit Aaron when he was little?

A: According to an interview with the British teen magazine, *BIG!*, yes. "I was bitten by a garden snake," Aaron recalled. "I was prodding it with a stick and it just turned around and bit me on the arm! I screamed because I remembered seeing someone on the TV who sucked poison out of his arm, so I tried to do that too. My dad ran up to me and said that the snake wasn't poisonous, so I was safe. But for a few minutes I thought I was going to die. Then Angel started trying to make it bite her so she could be the same as me!"

37. What toothpaste does Aaron use?

A: "Rembrandt," Aaron told *Smash Hits* magazine. "I brush my teeth three times a day . . . well, I try to!"

38: What was the most embarrassing thing that happened to Aaron?

A: "I tripped onstage over a monitor and fell face first into the crowd," Aaron revealed in a *TeenHollywood* Internet chat. "[Another time] a speaker fell on me during the Nickelodeon tour [last] summer. It was a HUGE speaker. It felt like it broke my arm, but it didn't. I had a bruise for weeks!"

39. What's the funniest question Aaron has ever been asked?

A: "I was once asked if I sang in the shower — that was a funny question," Aaron said in an Internet chat.

40. What's the weirdest thing Aaron has ever eaten?

A: "I think octopus," Aaron told *SuperTeen*. "I like to eat squid and octopus and sardines on crackers."

41. Does Aaron mind it when reporters ask him about Nick?

A: No way! "It's fun talking about him so I can tell on him and stuff," Aaron told *Top of the Pops Magazine*. "Like the last time he was in trouble for not tidying his room. It was at Christmas and he wanted to go play basketball, but my dad grounded him. He was mad!"

42: What's the best advice Aaron's mom ever gave him?

A: "She told me to always stay myself, and to always be me," Aaron to Scholastic magazines. "Never change. Always be who I am."

43. Does Aaron attend a regular school now?

A: No, he's home-schooled. "I have a tutor who comes out on the road with me," he told *TeenBeat* magazine. "Sometimes it gets a little annoying because when you're really tired you say to yourself, 'Oh, I don't want to do schooling.' But it's really important."

44. Do Nick and Aaron ever get into fights?

A: "Nick and I are real close — he's my best friend," Aaron told an Australian teen magazine reporter. "We argue sometimes, of course — we're brothers! The worst thing is that [when we argue], I get annoyed and try to hit him. But he just laughs at me and I get more annoyed. It doesn't happen all the time though — mostly we just play together and he buys me toys and stuff. Once, though, I told Nick there was a present for him in his room, then locked him in there for an hour. He was mad!"

45: When Aaron and Angel were little, did their mom dress them alike?

A: "Yes," Aaron revealed in a *Live & Kicking* interview. "But she [wore] pink and I [wore] blue."

46. Does Aaron get butterflies before he performs?

A: "I get a little bit nervous before I go onstage," he told *Smash Hits* magazine. "But I'm usually okay."

47. Does the crowd of fans ever scare Aaron when they surround him?

A: Sometimes it does get a little risky, but since he practically grew up watching Nick and the Backstreet Boys in similar situations, Aaron has learned to deal with it. However, he did tell *TeenBeat* magazine about one incident that he'll never forget. "When I was in Denmark, there was a near riot. We were driving through this crowd and the car was surrounded by girls. We couldn't move and it was something of a problem. We couldn't do a signing because there were so many girls there. Sometimes I get a little bit scared because I'm afraid they may break the windows."

48. Does it ever bother Aaron to be known as "Nick Carter's little brother"?

A: "I don't mind being known as Nick Carter's [little] brother," Aaron told the European magazine *U*, "but I [like] being noticed as myself, too."

49. Are Aaron's mom and dad good singers?

A: Aaron revealed in a Zoog Disney chat that his mom "sings in the shower! My grandpa, on my mom's side, was a singer, too. I think that's where I get my singing from."

50. What does love mean to Aaron?

A: Aaron explained in an interview on the website www.carterplanet.com, "Love is when you care about somebody, where you're there for somebody 24–7, like my parents. That's how it is. Sometimes when someone really likes somebody, they'll say, 'I love you, I love you!' But they don't really love them; it's just puppy love. Love is totally different from puppy love. Love is so different from any kind of feeling you've ever had. I mean, I haven't experienced it yet."

51. How do audiences around the world differ?

A: "The audiences in Germany are more hyper than they are in the United States," Aaron told *U* magazine. "The fans are kind of crazy over there. They give you all kinds of stuff like jewelry, shampoo, [and] cologne. In Malaysia, they gave me real live turtles and parakeets onstage! They were flying all around and the turtles were crawling all over the stage."

52. What's under Aaron's bed?

A: "There's a painting that Nick did — his very first one," Aaron told *Top of the Pops* magazine.

53. If Aaron could be a Beanie Baby, which one would he be?

A: "I'd want to be Britannia Bear," Aaron is quoted in *The Little Prince of Pop*. "She's special. You know she's only sold in England. She doesn't feel rough like some of the others. Her coat is soft, just like velvet. I love to touch her fur."

CHAPTER 9
Carter Family Reunion

At home with the Carters is an experience to remember. Something is always going on. Music is playing. People are laughing. Dogs are barking. Guests are splashing around in the pool. It's nonstop energy, movement, and electricity!

Actually the family — when they aren't traveling around the world on concert tours — is bi-coastal. The Carters kept their home in Florida even when they bought a beautiful ranch in southern California. Located up in the hills, the Carters named their new home Heaven's Gate. Aaron particularly likes the back-to-nature atmosphere of it. He loves exploring the hills with his dad, especially when they come across a wild boar or coyote — as long as its far, far away.

According to Jane in her book on Aaron, *The Little Prince of Pop*, Aaron's blossoming career had a *lot* to do with them choosing to relocate in southern California. "[It] was the best choice for Aaron," Jane wrote. "It included Los Angeles, where opportunities abounded for TV, movies, and even recording. Aaron says he loves it because 'It's just two minutes from the beach! And I can ride my XR80 motorcycle up in the Mojave Desert. I can run outside and climb down into hills filled with crystals.'"

Of course, Aaron loves to fly back to Florida too. When he's there, he either stays at his family's home, or bunks down at Nick's new home overlooking the water just outside of Tampa Bay. When he's at Nick's, Aaron plays with his big brother's two pug dogs, Mikey and Huston.

Leslie Carter, New Kid on the Block

Well, now that Nick and Aaron are both superstars, it's not so surprising that *another* Carter is on the verge of breaking into the limelight. This time, it's sister Leslie. After watching her brothers have all the fun, fourteen-year-old Leslie decided she wanted to get in on the act too!

Signed to Hollywood Records, Leslie released her first single, "I Want to Hear It from You" on June 6, 2000, which just happened to be her fourteenth birthday! After that Leslie joined the 2000 Nickelodeon Tour and spent the summer traveling across the U.S. In her record label biography, Leslie says, "This is something I want for myself. I want to be an entertainer. I want to do it all: singing, dancing, acting — it's all a part of me."

Who could doubt that — after all, Leslie is a Carter!

A Looky-Look at Leslie
Birthdate: June 6, 1986
Birthplace: Tampa, Florida
Nickname: Les, Lessie
Hair: Light brown with blond highlights
Eyes: Blue
Height: 5'5"
Righty or Lefty: She is left-handed
Instruments: Guitar and clarinet
Hobby: The martial art of Tae Kwon Do — she has an orange belt
Worst Habit: She says she bites her nails.
Biggest Fear: Roller coasters
Fave Soda: Coca-Cola
Fave Food: Pizza
Fave Animal: Horse
Fave Musical Artists: Jewel and Backstreet Boys
Fave Type of Music: Pop and R&B
Fave Actor: Leonardo DiCaprio

Fave Actress: Drew Barrymore
Fave Car: Corvette
Fave Holiday: Christmas
Fave Color: Green
Official Website: www.lesliecarter.com

Family Fun: The Carter Clan Spill the Beans on Each Other!

AARON

On Twin Sister Angel: "She's the complete opposite of me. She's very calm and since she was born one minute before me, she always looks after me like a mother goose."

On Big Brother Nick: "Out of all the pop stars I've met, Nick is my biggest idol because he's my brother and he always stands up for me."

On Sister Leslie: "Leslie has a Jewel kind of sound — and LeAnn Rimes."

ANGEL

On Being Nick and Aaron's Sister: "It's okay. But because I knew them before all this started, I don't think of them as being really, really famous. It was weird at first, but we've all got used to it now. . . . Nick's not at home much, but he still acts the same. Aaron is still a bit of a goofball."

LESLIE

On Her Childhood and Big Brother Nick: "I was unpopular in elementary school. Kids made fun of me. They teased me and called me a liar because they didn't believe Nick was my brother. . . . [But] Nick helped me a lot. Even though he's been real busy on tour, he always encourages me and makes me laugh."

B.J.

On Aaron: "I still can't believe how famous he is! It's great! *Surfin' USA* is definitely my fave of Aaron's videos."

NICK

On Family Time: "It's so nice to get some time at home. I love being on the road, but I miss my family."

On Aaron's At-Home Personality: "He's a little blond dancing fool and singing fool. Basically that's what he is."

On Aaron Being on the Road with BSB: "I think it's great because we've [been able to spend] a lot more time together than we usually have. I've been traveling everywhere and so has [Aaron], so we really hadn't been able to catch up with each other. It's really cool. I love him. He's my little brother."

On Aaron Being in Show Business: "I worry about my brother because it's a really hard business. We have to take a lot of pressure and it takes its toll. People tend to look at us and say that we are perfect — we're not. We've been through a lot of stress and a lot of it has to do with this business. What am I to think when someone Aaron's age comes into the business. . . . I personally would rather he didn't get involved in this, but it's his life. It's not up to me."

On Leslie's Singing Career: "Leslie has one of the best country music voices I've heard. . . . I've already written a song for her."

DAD BOB

On Carter Family Life: "Everything's the same at home as it always was . . . almost! Nick and Aaron aren't stars here, we're still the same old Carter family."

On Aaron: "Aaron is very quick, with an imaginative mind and he's smart. . . . Aaron is a natural actor, comedian, and also a dramatic talent. . . . Aaron's outgoing, maybe more than Nick, and he's also a bit more aggressive."

On the Relationship Between Aaron and Nick: "Nick and Aaron are very close and love each other a lot. Nick worries about Aaron and gives him advice."

MOM JANE

On Why She Wrote the Book *The Heart and Soul of Nick Carter — Secrets Only a Mother Knows*: "I was on tour with the boys and saw how interested the fans were in Nick. I felt this was the way to give the fans an in-depth look into who Nick really is."

On Nick and Aaron's Musical Talents: "Aaron's learning guitar. Nick learned vocal and he taught himself the drums. When Nick is home, you always know it because the drums are, like, bam bam bam! It's crazy."

On Aaron as a Little Boy: "He was a little mischievous. He's a lot more outgoing than Nick and he gets into a lot more trouble than Nick did, but of course, Nick got into his share, too."

On How Nick and Aaron Make Her Laugh: "Whenever Nick sees me, he smiles and says [in a high squeaky voice], 'Mama!' Aaron's forever doing cartwheels — that makes me laugh. He's a charmer too and good at changing the subject when he thinks he's in trouble. It's kinda cute because he thinks he's pulling a fast one. Oh, I could go on forever . . . let's just say I'm really proud of them both!"

On Parenting Famous Stars: "[Bob and I are] parents. We don't control our children; we guide them. Everybody has rules to survive by. They may get grounded or told to go to their rooms, but not often at all because they are really great kids."

CHAPTER 10

Reach Out to Aaron

Going Postal (snail mail)
Record Company:
Aaron Carter
c/o Jive Records
137–139 West 25th Street
New York, NY 10001

Surf's Up (online)
Official Aaron Carter Website: www.aaroncarterlpop.com
Official Aaron Carter E-Mail (for your own personal Aaron
Carter e-mail): yourname@aaroncarter.com
Official General Website Info E-Mail:
info@carterworld.cjb.net
News & TV Appearances E-Mail: news@carterworld.cjb.net

Aaron Carter Fan Club Info
Official Online Fan Club: www.aaroncarter1pop.com
Official U.S. Fan Club:
Aaron Carter
P.O. Box 1412
Ruskin, FL 33570

International Fan Clubs:
Aaron Carter Fan Info
P.O. Box 8157
London W2 3GZ
England

Aaron Carter Fan Club
P.O. Box 0617
94307 Straubing
Germany

CHAPTER 11

Discography

Aaron Carter (1997)

Trans Continental Records/Edel America, Inc.

Tracks

"I Will Be Yours"
"Crazy Little Party Girl"
"One Bad Apple"
"I'm Gonna Miss You Forever"
"Tell Me How To Make You Smile"
"Shake It"
"Please Don't Go Girl"
"Get Wild"
"I'd Do Anything"
"Ain't That Cute"

"Crush on You"
"Swing It Out"

European Singles (1997–1999)

"Crush on You"
"Crazy Little Party Girl"
"I'm Gonna Miss You Forever"
"Surfin' USA"
"Shake It"

Aaron Carter Surfin' USA (1999)

Trans Continental Records/Edel America, Inc.
(EP released in the United States)

Tracks

"Surfin' USA"
"Shake It"
"Crush on You"
"Crazy Little Party Girl"
"I'm Gonna Miss You Forever"
Bravo All Stars — "Let The Music Heal Your Soul" (featuring Aaron Carter, Backstreet Boys, 'N Sync, Blumchen, The Boyz, Gil, Mr. President, The Moffatts, R 'N' G, Scooter, and Sqeezer)

Single by the "Bravo All Stars"

Benefit for the Nordoff-Robbins Music Therapy Foundation
"Let The Music Heal Your Soul"

Pokémon: The First Movie soundtrack

WEA/Atlantic Records 1999
"Have Some Fun with the Funk"

Aaron's Party (Come Get It)

Jive Records (2000)

Tracks

"Introduction: Come to the Party"
"Aaron's Party (Come Get It)"
"I Want Candy"
"Bounce"
"My Internet Girl"
"The Clapping Song"
"Iko Iko"
"Real Good Time"
"Tell Me What You Want"
"Jump Jump"
"Girl You Shine"

Music Awards

1998: British Edition of *Guinness Book of World Records* entry for being the youngest singer to have the most consecutive Top 10 hits in England.

1998: two Golden Ottos from *BRAVO* magazine for top entertainer of the year in Germany and Spain.

1998: British teen magazines *Popcorn* and *Pop/Rocky* named Aaron the "Best Singer of the Year."

1998: Aaron's European debut album, *Aaron Carter,* went gold in twelve countries and platinum in Japan.

Fun Facts

On Aaron's *Aaron Carter* album, brother Nick Carter sang background vocals on "Please Don't Go Girl."

"Please Don't Go Girl" was written by Maurice Starr, the man who put together New Edition and New Kids on the Block.

"Ain't That Cute," another song from *Aaron Carter,* was written by Backstreet Boys Nick Carter and Brian Littrell.

Aaron's sister Angel appeared in the video for "Shake It."